Exile in the Stars

*

A BOOK OF HOURS
FOR THE FIRST SUNDAY
IN ADVENT

THE MACMILLAN COMPANY
NEW YORK · BOSTON · CHICAGO
DALLAS · ATLANTA · SAN FRANCISCO

MACMILLAN AND CO., LIMITED
LONDON · BOMBAY · CALCUTTA
MADRAS · MELBOURNE

THE MACMILLAN COMPANY
OF CANADA, LIMITED
TORONTO

Exile in the Stars

A BOOK OF HOURS
FOR THE FIRST SUNDAY
IN ADVENT

by James J. Donohue

1946

THE MACMILLAN COMPANY · NEW YORK

NIHIL OBSTAT

Arthur J. Scanlan, S.T.D.
Censor Librorum

IMPRIMATUR

✠ *Francis J. Spellman, D.D.*
Archbishop, New York

New York, June 11, 1945

Copyright, 1945, by
THE MACMILLAN COMPANY

———

———

Second Printing

PRINTED IN THE UNITED STATES OF AMERICA
BY THE VAIL-BALLOU PRESS, INC., BINGHAMTON, N. Y.

CONTENTS

CONTENTS

BEFORE THE HOURS

Open, O God, this stubborn mouth
  To bless Thy holy name.
Nourish no vigil planets in the south,
  Candle no noonday flame,
Suffer no beast attendants at the throne,
  Dower no birds with tongue,
But let the Office be by us alone
  Tended and sung.
Clean the dark thought and take away—
  Take what is empty and unwhole
Take what is twisted and astray,
  Take what is foreign to a soul.
Clean the dark mansion, Lord,
  Clay and unkept:
Make it a habitation for the Word,
  Garnished and swept.
Brighten my mind to read,
  Kindle my love to hold—
Equal and open, eager and agreed
  To what the Hours unfold.
Now what is truth be said,
  Now what is praise be heard,
Now what is right be led
  Through Jesus Christ our Lord.
                              Amen.

This is Thy Son, O Father:
  Though there are some to doubt Him,

Wherever beggars gather
    They shall not pray without Him.
Begging (not once) they found Him,
    Praying (though not as I),
Pleading from mountains: and around Him
    All was not sky,
But (whether hope or fear)
    Something of earth was blended.
I will go guided here,
    Meaning as He intended.

A Book of Hours

FOR THE FIRST SUNDAY IN ADVENT
incipit

MATINS

Versicle	Open, O Lord, my lips to pray.
	What shall my mouth proclaim?
Response	What shall the morning find to say
	Except Thy holy name?

INVITATORY

*Come and adore the Lord, hurry and praise
**God in the strange beginning of His ways.
   Not in the reach of His priority,
     Not the All-present Being:
   The mystery before exteriority
     Awaits our wonder and escapes our seeing.
      Not the white arc: rather the outward rays;
     *Come and adore the Lord, hurry and praise.
   Not when there was no earth to keep in hand:
     But when the bounds were drawn;
   After created ocean, founded land,
     Peaks to look down upon;
      Eternity offset by nights and days;
     **God in the strange beginning of His ways.
   Not for the moment of His isolation:
     But for the day that took

3

Us for His people and His occupation,
   Lambs of His flock.
      Rejoice to God and stand before His face;
      *Come and adore the Lord, hurry and praise.
Not in His prime: rather in our beginning,
   After there first was scorn,
After confession came and psalms and sinning,
   After the gods were born.
*Come and adore the Lord, hurry and praise
**God in the strange beginning of His ways.

H<small>YMN</small>

Indulgent Maker of the light
   And Giver still of day to earth,
Who wrote in light when it was new
   First inkling of a world in birth,

Who interlocking dawn with dusk
   Made creatures call the hours *Day*,
Black chaos closes in again:
   God hear us, for in tears we pray.

Black chaos closes in again,
   And Thy creation is unmade
Whenever we to heart's desire
   Re-order courses Thou hast laid.

Black chaos closes in again
   When fettered love and heavy head
Renounces being and contrives
   Primeval nothingness instead.

Father unborn and unobeyed,
   Son and Redeemer dead in vain,
Spirit and unregarded Fire,
   Black chaos closes in again.
                    Amen.

4

THE FIRST NOCTURN

Antiphon 1. God said: "Let there be light——

"This is for souls. Even some dark creation
Were room enough for *dust* to check and speed—
Lock and unleash. Some dimmer revelation
Were ample for blind flesh to hurt and breed.
This is for souls. But, so no link of being
May snarl uneven in My measured chain,
On belly, wing, and claw go blest with seeing
Things of no vision higher than a brain.
This is for souls, that—from the seeming vapor
Of galaxy to the apparent crust
Of atom—souls may read by star or taper
The wonder of their marriage to the dust.
　　This is the first-born of My ways with men
　　And with the last-born soul goes dark again."

Ant. God said: "Let there be light." And light was
　　made.
Ant. 2. God said: "Let there be sky——

"This is for poets. . . . Reasoner and empiric,
Measure this vault deep as the suns aspire,
Broaden cónclusions coldly in your pyrrhic
Conquest of compass at the price of fire.
Which of you dare proclaim what bitter waters
This shell divides from the sweet nether rain,
What suction tenses or what deluge batters
The limits that you fix or ascertain?
Not only where the Bear remotely raises
His vaguest nebula, but here upon
Earth-rind and sea-film, cell-wall, skin of faces,
Shingle, and shroud, the firmament is drawn.
　　Wisdom will tell where surface bends and why,
　　But only poets see behind the sky."

Ant. God said: "Let there be sky." And He made a
   vault.
Ant. 3. God said: "Let the dry land appear——

"This is for wanderers. . . . Abiders, dwellers,
The wheat will quicken and the apples keep,
The wine will ripen in your careful cellars,
And you will stir a little in your sleep.
Suffer the vagrant mildly in your orchard:
Whether the clerk escaping through the corn,
Or roofless stray, or tented rover tortured
By blood of which discovery is born.
Not many glimpse the roofs beyond Sahara,
Recover cities or uncharted men,
Pioneer tundra, jungle, or sierra:
But every boy will dream of Darien.
   Vagabonds shall possess the land: to roam
   And teach you that the earth is not your home."

Ant. God said: "Let the dry land appear." And it
   was so.

V.   Looking I saw the light and sky and earth.
R.   And His dark beauty stood unhidden forth.

———————

Absolution
Forgive us, Father, take our praise,
Who with the Son and Spirit made the light
The strange beginning of Thy ways.
                              Amen.

Blessing 1
Eternal Fender of the night,
Be Thou the Keeper of my days,
Who with the Son and Spirit made the light.
                              Amen.

6

BEGINS THE BOOK OF GENESIS:
In the beginning God made
   Heaven and earth: earth was empty,
Earth was void, and darkness
   Was on the face of the sky-gulf
[*this was water*]: the Breath
   Of God moved over the water.
"Let there be light," He said,
   And light was made: He saw it—
Saw it that it was good,
   And divided the light from the darkness.
Light He called *Day* and darkness *Night*.
   (Evening and morning: the first day).
"Be there a vault," He said,
   "In the middle of the waters:
Let it roof water from water—
   Water above from water below."
It was done and He called the vault *Sky*.
   (Evening and morning: the second day).
"Let all the waters," He said,
   "That are under the vault of heaven
Flock in one place together,
   And let the dry land appear."
It was so and He called the land *Earth*,
   But the flocking of waters *Ocean*.
"Let the earth sprout," He said,
   "Plants that are green and seed-making,
Food-bearing wood making fruit
   With seed in it after its likeness."
It was so and He saw they were good.
   (Evening and morning: the third day).

R.   I see the glory of God, all my life I have seen it.
       I see God in the light, I see God in the darkness.

*I will walk before God, I will herald Him crying:

**If This be not God, unmake the light from the sky-
vault,

***Unbend the arch of heaven, confuse the earth and the
ocean.

V. We are sons of the earth, we are saints, we are sinners.

*We will walk before God, we will herald Him crying.

V. Where there are sheep is a shepherd, where there are
strays is a seeker:

**If This be not God, unmake the light from the sky-
vault.

V. If we obey unobserved, if we sin unattended,

***Unbend the arch of heaven, confuse the earth and the
ocean.

V. Glory be to the Father, the Son, and the Holy Spirit.

R. I see the glory of God, all my life I have seen it.

I see God in the light, I see God in the darkness.

I will walk before God, I will herald Him crying:

If This be not God, unmake the light from the sky-
vault,

Unbend the arch of heaven, confuse the earth and the
ocean.

Blessing 2
First Image of the Father's inward gaze,
First Word and only ever uttered right,
Help us, Redeemer, take our praise.
Amen.

LESSON TWO

"Let there be lamps," God said,
    "Lamps in the vault of heaven,
Signals of dates and seasons,
    To light the earth." And He made them:
Two great lamps and the stars.
    (Evening and morning: the fourth day).

8

"Let the sea spawn," He said,
    And He created monsters
And everything creeping alive
    Such as the waters engender,
And things flying over the land.
    And He spoke them His blessing, saying:
"Increase and multiply!"
    (Evening and morning: the fifth day).

R.   I see the glory of God: God in the lamps of the sky-
        vault,
    God in wings over land, God in the teem of the sea-
        spawn.
    *Every tribe sees God, every people and language.
V.   We see no likelihood that the sight of God shall di-
        minish.
    We see no likelihood that the kingdom of God shall be
        shaken.
    *Every tribe sees God, every people and language.

Blessing 3
Untangle, Spirit, and make bright
The strange beginning of Thy ways
To heavy head and backward sight.
                    Amen.

LESSON THREE

"Let the earth litter," God said,
    "Cattle and beast and reptile.
Let Us make man to Our likeness."
    And God made man to His image,
Made him to image of God,
    Man and woman He made them.
"Increase and multiply,"
    He spoke them His blessing saying,
"People the earth and tame it,

9

Master the animal creature.
Here I give plant and tree
    To you and your brutes for eating."
He saw they were all very good.
    (Evening and morning: the sixth day).
Thus were heaven and earth
    Finished and all their appointments.
But God on the seventh day
    Fulfilled the work and rested,
Rested the seventh day,
    Blest it and made it holy,
Because on the seventh day
    He desisted. [*This is the Sabbath*].

R. Brutes are sent through the earth to tell the power and
the glory.

Men are sent through the earth to see the power and
the glory.

*There is a sabbath from power, there is no sabbath from
glory.

V. We will take rest of one kind, but another rest is denied us:

*There is a sabbath from power, there is no sabbath from
glory.

V. Glory be to the Father, the Son, and the Holy Spirit.

*There is a sabbath from power, there is no sabbath from
glory.

THE SECOND NOCTURN

Ant. 4. God made the sun and said:

"This is for workers. I prepare the acres,
Provision quarries, nurse the timber lands,
But after time and weather come the makers,
Concluding My creation with their hands.
Sooner than grass can claim the place of battle,
The strong ones of the earth go toiling by,
Walking the graves erect behind their cattle,
Planting and reaping where the others lie.
After the desert chokes the wit and laughter,
The grinding wind spares hammer-marks on stones:
In the true line of wall and painted rafter
The cunning slave outlives his master's bones.
   There is rest sometimes in the night and rain,
   But with the sun the makers rise again."

Ant. God made the sun and said: "Rule the day."
Ant. 5. God made the moon and said:

"This is for lovers. Let there be truce to thunder
Sometimes and pause upon the wet monsoon,
Till consecration of a poet's blunder
Lets lovers in their hour possess the moon.
Not many landscapes, not many kinds of weather,
But valley vistas laced with light and shade,
Widening waters shot with the sky together
Will fit the words and music that are made.

11

Let there be lamplight through the garden lancing,
Let there be wine and laughter in the hall,
Let the night pulse with silver and the glancing
Of briar noises from the arbor wall.
    And for their innocence they shall entreat
    A Woman with the moon beneath her feet."

Ant. God made the moon and said: "Rule the night."
Ant. 6. God made the stars and said:

"This is for wise men. Clipper and cruiser reckon
Midnight by Vega climbing in the spars,
Vigilant Bear and Dragon chart and beckon
Sailors, but only wise men track the stars.
Watch the empiric, you that put faith in counting,
Number the suns which prowl beyond Altair:
You that prize reason out of eyesight mounting,
See the dark star-dust hunted to its lair.
To these, if any, heaven shows the glory,
And sky declares the work, and day has word
For day, and night for other night has story
That needs no speech or language to be heard.
    Not only three come star-led to My birth:
    The sound of suns goes to the end of earth."

Ant. God made the stars and said: "Signals of dates and
    seasons."

V.   I will arise at midnight to confess Thee,
R.   Who made the sun and moon and stars profess Thee.

    Absolution
    Be Thou my help and mercy, God the Son,
    Who keep the heavens night and day,
    With Father and the Spirit Three in One.
                    Amen.

Blessing 4
Father and Guide to stars and feet astray,
Order the orbit I must run,
Who keep the heavens night and day.
                              Amen.

LESSON FOUR

BEGINS THE PRAISE OF ENGINEERS:
I sometimes think that mountains are not worth
The singing. Yes, I know how long the world
Smoldered at heart, I know the sudden surge
Squandering sunshine hoarded from the spume
Of seething galaxies, irreparable
Heartbreak of shrieking atoms, rigid jars
Wringing the iron veins and ecstasy
Grinding complaining bones of stony deeps,
Hot thrust and thaw of granite-smothered fires,
And stiff earth-stirrings—till the tortured land
Writhed into hills. Mountains do this: they shout
Above their silence brute omnipotence,
And men unwilling suddenly see God.

R.   I sometimes think that mountains are not worth
       The singing, but they argue in their birth
      *And men unwilling suddenly see God.
V.   Yes, logic in the ecstasy of earth,
      *And men unwilling suddenly see God.

Blessing 5
In every scheme and action done,
In all omission and delay,
Be Thou my help and mercy, God the Son.
                              Amen.

And yet—God has done better things. There is
A wonder in the hills: someone has dared
To hurt their immortality, to drown
Their chasm-spruces under upstart lakes,
Lakes that the sun had never looked upon
Till he was old, to loop their stubborn crags
And tangle up their pines with creeping threads
Of gray, to scar them red with raw ravines
Even where their toughest spurs had shouldered off
The futile foam of fifty million years.
"A giant has been here, some monster power
More than the mountains!" If you but knew, a child
With tiny hands has done these things in play.

R.   God has done better things: the mountains change,
    *A child with tiny hands has done the thing in play.
V.   No giant has been here to crack the range,
    *A child with tiny hands has done the thing in play.

Blessing 6
Spirit, accessible to all who pray,
With Son and Father Three in One,
Touch with Thy Fire my erring way.
                        Amen.

LESSON SIX

I wonder if he laughed or wept to see
His work; perhaps he was too rapt for tears
Or laughter even, laboring here half-smiling.
One thing I know: he panted at the task,
As children will in play; to gouge these hills
His fingers must have bled; he must have seen
Death in this mountain-taming. But he knew
The weaknesses of granite; he was wise

14

To burrow craftily the ringing flanks
Of peaks too tall to tumble, wise to leap
Boldly the gorge of gulfs too deep to fill—
Tireless as icy wind whetting the range,
Reckless of danger as a footed tree
Creeping the precipice. Is he a fool
Not knowing or a jester not to care
That mountains are his masters? So he lays
Heavy upon the hills his little hands
And breaks them to his glory and to God.

R.   Suddenly sometimes men unwilling see
       The logic of the earth's stiff ecstasy,
    *But this I know: upon the mountain lands
   **Glory is written in the press of hands.
V.   The hills will argue and the wise man hear it,
    *But this I know: upon the mountain lands
V.   Glory to Father, Son, and Holy Spirit,
   **Glory is written in the press of hands.

THE THIRD NOCTURN

Ant. 7. God made the spawn of the sea and said:

"This is for fishers. Pilots at their stations
Curse and outrun the trawler down to lee,
But fishers have the oldest kind of patience
And the primeval science of the sea.
They sharpen eyes upon the sea and sky light,
They harden hands upon the polished oar,
Then silent as their fathers, dawn or twilight,
They fail of rendezvous with ship or shore.
But when false tears secure the lamb from slaughter
And anxious merchants lock the tools away,
Free yellow sails shall arrow fenceless water
Over old shallows after ancient prey.
   Bear the sea stoutly, heave the nets again,
   Against the day I need fishers of men."

Ant. God made the spawn of the sea and said: "Fill
   the waters."
Ant. 8. God made the beast of the earth and said:

"This is for herders. Some will break wild horses,
Ride the dawn skyline black against the east,
Bend the stampede of roan insensate forces,
And file like gods above the herded beast.
Some will hold barns against December's fury
And warm the houses where their fathers slept.
Turn from the puzzled epitaph of glory

16

And write of these: *They builded and they kept.*
And some will haunt with sheep the lonely places,
Loving few mountainsides and many stars,
Till the dumb ranges crane conversant faces
At the shrill arc of Jupiter and Mars.
  So, shepherds will see angels fanning down,
  Singing mad words above the heedless town."

Ant. God made the beast of the earth and said: "Fill
    the land."
Ant. 9. God made the sabbath:

"This is for clay. Six mornings of creation
Will satisfy the plans I have for dust,
And flesh will share My moment of cessation
Though engines idle and the weapons rust.
This is for clay. Not fire shall outburn *spirit,*
Your pride is scarcely shorter than My law:
Nor light outshine the vision that can bear it,
I am the only measure of your awe.
There is a time for recess, time for sleeping,
Holiday, intermission, and parole;
There is a pause from planting, rest from reaping:
This is for clay—no respite for the soul.
  Cain in his stronghold is not fancy-free,
  Nor shall Augustine ever rest in Me."

Ant. God made the sabbath, and He rested.

V.   Now God is templed in His holy place,
R.   Peoples and lands be still before His face.

Absolution
Spirit, from bond of sin untie us,
Forgiveness is Thy mercy and Thy might;
With Son and Father sanctify us.
                    Amen.

Blessing 7
Father, the Gospel is our light;
Pardon our vision, rectify us,
Forgiveness is Thy mercy and Thy might.
                                    Amen.

LESSON SEVEN

READING OF THE HOLY GOSPEL
   ACCORDING TO MATTHEW:
   Chapter 18, 1–10:
In that hour, the disciples
Came to Jesus, saying:
"Who do you think is greater
In the kingdom of heaven?"
AND FURTHER WORDS OF THIS GOSPEL.

FOR HOMILY BEGINS THE PRAISE OF ANGELS:
Come let us praise, of the elder creation,
Terrible brothers before us in birth:
Unmeasured presences, love without passion,
Clockless endurances, effortless truth:
Thurifers and Intuitions,
Monstrances, Plenipotentiaries,
Principalities, Dominations,
Faculties, Captains, and Emissaries.
Birth and instant adult fixation,
All were tested and some were proven,
Momently wheeling from introspection
To face the Father Who is in heaven.

R.   This is their breathing, burning word:
          *"All the earth is full of His glory—
V.   Holy, holy, holy Lord,
          *All the earth is full of His glory."

Lesson Eight

But the Day-Star said in the hour of his rising:
"I will ascend to the utter sphere,
Sit above stars of God's devising,
Fix on the peak and pole of the year.
The zenith I make for my enterprising
Is higher than orbit, vapor, and clod,
And the planets of my evangelizing
Are more than the moons of the Most High God."
But the arc of his apostatizing
Slanted and broke on the floor of hell,
And the satellites of his scandalizing
Abyssward bolts of meteor fell.

R.   Day-Star, Day-Star, fallen from morning,
        *Day-Star, risen before the Sun.
V.   Day-Star, Day-Star, earthward burning,
        *Day-Star, risen before the Sun.

Lesson Nine

And the Day-Star said in the hour of his setting:
"I have committed war in the sky,
Vaulted the orbit of my begetting
For a track too steep and a place too high,

19

And learnt by trial of Michael-meeting
What house is shuttered against my sway,
What recompense for my tall unseating
Is mine on the underside of day.
But I know there are upstart planets waiting
For path to follow and sun to seize,
And I will bend them gravitating
Upon the pole of antipodes."

R.   This is that dragon, ancient foeman,
        Liar, seducer of man and woman,
     *Serpent, cockle, wicked leaven,
    **His place is found no more in heaven.
V.   This is that slanderer unwearied,
     *Serpent, cockle, wicked leaven.
V.   Glory to Father, Son, and Spirit:
   **His place is found no more in heaven.

LAUDS

Ant. 1. These are the generations of the stars:

There are four rivers in the misty motion
That bends the shoreless sky-gulf like an eel:
Not onward, streamlike, nor to any ocean,
But inward pool on pool the rivers reel.
For one reposes throbbing, welling, shifting
Heaven on heaven, tangent to no bed;
One tumbles constellations edgelong-drifting
By star-banks laggard, cross-drawn, counter-fed;
One brushes stars on some black pivot swirling
Or blasting from some fiery inner one;
One drives my garden and the others hurling
Half-centered on the kindness of the sun.
    Fools say these rivers are 'too big and fine'
    To focus on one garden small as mine.

Ant. These are the generations of the stars before
      there were wise men.
Ant. 2. These are the generations of the earth:

There are four rivers in the cunning weather
That shapes the earth from substance of the sun:
Not four abreast, but in one file together,
In sequel or alloy, the rivers run.
River of fire now only smolders, flashes
Beneath the channel where it flamed and fell,
But all our walking is upon its ashes—

Our footsteps jar the vibrant tides of hell;
River of rock we darkly guess at, shaken
Sometimes when hidden granite crawls aloud;
River of wind we taste on every waking;
River of rain we smell in every cloud.
    These rivers have flowed patiently and far
    To wrest my garden from a barren star.

Ant. These are the generations of the earth before
    there were wanderers.
Ant. 3. These are the generations of cattle:

There are four rivers in the bestiary
That peoples earth before descent of man:
Not inward on one current, tributary,
But outward, delta-wise, the rivers fan.
One is the rooted green of field or fallow,
Food-bearing wood and fruit-producing seed;
One is the sunken clan of deep or shallow,
Monster and minim which the waters breed;
One is the lineage of wind-compellers,
Wings under sky and wings above the earth;
And one is dynasty of surface-dwellers,
Stalker or prey according to its birth.
    In their increase they let my garden lie
    Lonely and empty where they multiply.

Ant. These are the generations of cattle before
    there were herders.
Ant. 4. And there was not a man.

Canticle to Loneliness

Archangel of Immensity, whose foot
Overtrod empty earth and left no sign
Before we came to trim the savage vine,

Tame the mad herd, and harvest the wild fruit,
Yours is the ocean now, heather and butte,
Swampland and pole, desert and timberline,
And in the gulfy places that confine
The lonely stars your way is absolute.
    Are you for good or evil? Angry bird
    Tearing Prometheus and sad errantry
    Of Cain upstarting from the voice of God?
    Or nurse of men? as when Gotama heard
    Some of your silence and your company
    Nerved Moses' hand around that awful rod.

Ant. And there was not a man to till the earth.
Ant. 5. And God said:

"Our praise is certain in the pious forces
Which weave Our glory in the sunny skies,
Nor are the suns in their unfailing courses
Too proud to focus on one paradise.
Our praise is certain where the breakers smother
In foam and gale the golden ocean bar
Or ice and flame conspire with one another
To shape the garden from a barren star.
Our praise is certain in the thoughtless voices
And aimless ways of beast and bird, who die
With no tomorrow; but the garden poises
Lonely and empty while they multiply.
    Let Us give breath to clay and bear with blame
    To fill the garden with reluctant fame."

Ant. And God said: "Let Us make man."

LITTLE CHAPTER: *Genesis 2, 7–8:*

And the Lord God formed man
Of the slime of the earth
And breathed into his face

The breath of life,
And man became a living soul.
And the Lord God had planted
A garden of pleasure from the beginning
Where He placed man whom He had formed.

Hymn

Eternal Founder of the sky,
   The suns are numbered where they swing;
The very star-dust is not free
   To fall without Thy reckoning.

Carefully leaning long ago
   Among the labyrinth of night,
Thy questing finger found and kept
   One track secure, one planet bright.

Blind to the pattern earth described
   Pre-natal on the loom of space,
We only know we woke at dawn
   And felt Thy breath upon our face.

We know the garden of our prime
   Darkly in dreams and whisperings,
Remembering one boyhood hour
   Of wiser laughter, better things.

We know at noon the garden gone,
   The portal coldly crossed with bars:
Darkness is never far from day,
   And earth an exile in the stars.

Carefully bend as long ago
   Among Thy truer points of fire
And turn our outcast planet square
   Upon the land of our desire.

Father and Founder of the sky,
　　Only-begotten Truth and Light,
Spirit and kindly Beacon-Ray,
　　Bring us to Eden in the night.
Amen.

V.　　Boundless and beautiful the desert stood:
R.　　One well was peopled in the solitude.

Ant. God made a garden of pleasure.

CANTICLE TO EDEN

Guardian Cherub, Keeper of Paradise,
We once knew innocence beneath your wings
And happiness a moment under skies
Peopled with more than earth-returning things.
What are you guarding now? Unaltered springs
Feeding Euphrates still, where unexplored
The borealis of your falchion swings?
Or wilderness unworthy of your sword
Fallen on desert days, like us who knew the Lord?

Ant. God made a garden of pleasure, which we
　　remember.

Let us pray:
Gather and bring, we beseech Thee, Thy light to this riddle,
　　Redeemer:
How we came first to the garden and then to the garden of
　　earth,
And why the fair well in the desert is not the water of life;
Thou Who art Life, and one King, and one God with the
　　Father and Spirit,
World without end. *Amen.*

PRIME

HYMN

Daybreak is ancient out of mind,
    O God, the risen sun is old:
We have few memories of light
    And none of primal dark and cold.

Blind to the pattern earth described
    Pre-natal on the loom of space,
We only know we woke at dawn
    And felt Thy breath upon our face.

Instruct us that the breath is life,
    A virtue stinging through the slime,
Thinner than stresses in the void
    And stronger than the tides of time.

Instruct us that the breath is wise,
    Past shadows mounting to acquire
Profiling figures and possess
    In Thee the silhouetting Fire.

Instruct us that the breath is free,
    A spirit blowing where it will:
Unleash this wilful hunger, Lord,
    And bind it to Thy purpose still.

Untrammeled Father of the dawn,
    Wisdom and sole-begotten Son,
Spirit and Fountainhead of life,
    Brighten forever Three in One.
                Amen.

Ant. And man became.

Forget the scalpel: you will not dissever
This spirit from the flesh till flesh be clod—
This is the solid self, the live endeavor
That shapes the slime to image of its God.
Forget the eye: with lenses it will capture
No sight of aura in the brain or bone,
Nor naked look on ghost from pain or rapture,
Waking at midnight guilty and alone.
Forget the sword: you cannot kill your brother—
Meet face to face with any man you slay,
You only change that meeting for another,
And his the judgment on that second day.
    Eternity shall see and not survive
    Somewhere the substance of the soul alive.

Not undelighted in our cave we shelter,
But ravished with the pageant on the wall
And keen to ferret rhythm from the welter
Where blue on buff the lovely shadows fall.
Not ignorant of anything that paces
Opaque, behind, to interrupt the flame,
We know the guise of the profiling faces
And call each presence by its secret name.
Not comfortless, but with the hearth behind us
And light between the shadows, we aspire
To feign askance what face to face would blind us
The splendor of the silhouetting Fire.
    Thy creatures will ascend on wing and eye,
    But one shall set his feet upon the sky.

God, I could take some beast of Thine and measure
The fodder which divides him from the night,
Put price upon his energy and leisure,
Subtract his anguish from his brute delight.

Father, my loaves and flagons could be counted,
Labor and sleep be quoted at their worth,
Vision of star and hero be discounted
Against the woe of death and pang of birth.
But Judgment is one gift past calculation:
Hell is my chance to ratify, refuse;
Heaven is less my settled destination
Than goal not mine to earn but mine to choose.
   Despite of glory, if I am not free
   I know the measure of my debt to Thee.

Ant. And man became a living soul.

Little Chapter: *1 Timothy 1, 17:*

To the lord of the ages,
Immortal, unseen,
To the only God
Be honor and glory
Forever and ever.   *Amen.*

Little R.

   *Son of the living God, **such praise we owe to the Father.

V.   Because we are made to His likeness,
   **Such praise we owe to the Father.

V.   Glory be to the Father, the Son, and the Holy Spirit.
   *Son of the living God, **such praise we owe to the Father.

V.   Rise and instruct our praise, because He has made us spirits,

R.   Because He has made us wise, because He has made us choosers.

28

We name Thee Father in each prayer we make,
Believing that in Thee we rise and wake.
We praise the wonder, with each breaking day,
Of Thy first breath upon the sleeping clay;
We praise the favor, with the climbing sun,
Of weight to carry and a race to run;
We praise, with foresight of mortality,
Promise of sunset and of rest in Thee.
Thine be the glory: Thine is the Power that drew
The image first and makes the image new;
Thine be the glory: Thine is the Love that gave
Freemen their peril and redeems the slave;
Thine be the glory: Thine is the Fire and Light
That fled the sullied house and burns it white.

God is our Power: we confess aloud
That clay is heavy and the spirit proud;
God is our Prompter: He will not despise,
But shorten folly, for He made us wise;
God is our Savior: He will not decree
Silence of sinners, for He made us free.
Our prayer of praise is heard,
Our cry comes to the Lord.

Let us pray:
God the Father Almighty, Who hast neither shadow nor
season,
Who counted the arc of the sun as nothing before our begin-
ning,
Who woke us first in the dawn and bounded our day by the
sunset:
Save us today by Thy strength that we may not slope into evil
But up on the wings of Thy will; through Jesus Christ our
Redeemer,

Who is one Life, and one King, and one God with Thee and
   the Spirit,
World without end.   *Amen.*

———————

MARTYROLOGY

On the First Sunday of the Coming
   of Our Lord Jesus Christ,
This Pause in Our Prayer
   Is Made, to Remember:
Nahum the Prophet,
   buried in Begabar.
And, at Noyon,
   Loy the Bishop,
Wonderworker—
   the same holy man
Who teaches the tools
   of molder of metal,
      carver of gems.
At Rome, the passion
   of Bibiana Virgin,
Who under the wicked
   Emperor Julian
Died long smitten
   with leaden rods
      for the love of Christ.
On San-Chuan,
   an island of China,
Francis Xavier
   of the Company of Jesus,
Apostle of the Indies,
   remembered for miracles,
Remembered for graces,
   remembered for many
Who received the sign

of Christ at his lips—
The same holy man
  who is patron of preachers
That spread the faith
  afar among pagans.
And, in Judea,
  Saint Sophonias,
    Prophet of God.
At Imola, Peter
  Bishop of Ravenna,
Whose speech was called golden,
  saint and scholar.
And, at Nicomedia,
  the passion of Barbara,
Who under Maximin
  suffered shamefully,
Slain by the sword—
  the same holy Virgin
Is protector of towers
  and all who erect them,
All who inhabit them,
  all who destroy them;
Keeper of crucible,
  forge, and furnace;
Art of the architect;
  might of the mason;
Comfort of captive;
  guardian of gunner,
Grenadier, bomber,
  miner, sweeper,
Engineer, sapper,
  and dynamiter;
Shelter and shield
  in blast and volley,
Reef and avalanche,
  thunder and lightning,

and sudden death.
At Mutala, Sabbas,
 light of Palestine,
  defender of the faith.
At Myra in Lycia,
 Nicholas Bishop,
Who threw secret gifts
 in at the window
And flew from far
 for those that invoked him—
The same holy man
 is guard of Greece
And rampart of Russia,
 and taken for patron
By baker and brewer,
 merchant and lender;
The same who is saint
 of all that give presents
  in the name of Christ.
To the chair of Milan
 the ascent of Ambrose,
Doctor of the Church—
 the same holy man
Whose music is remembered
 in the kind of hymns
That we give to God,
 and who to Augustine
  was father in Christ.
The day which defined
 that high exception
From the fall of man
 whereby the Virgin
Mother Mary
 was conceived without stain
  of original sin.
And Elsewhere Others,

Many Martyrs,
Confessors of Virtue,
Holy Virgins.
Thanks Be to God.

The sleep of the saints
is a precious thing
in the sight of the Lord.

Without "Let us pray":
Mother conceived without sin and free from the curse of your
children,
Prophets of God and Martyrs, Confessors and Bishops and
Virgins:
Pray that subjection and death may bring us to living domin-
ion,
Healed and ordained by the Lord; for His is the Life and the
Kingdom,
World without end.   *Amen.*

Glory be to the Father, the Son, and the Holy Spirit,
As was in the beginning, is now, and shall be forever.
                                        Amen.

V.   Look to Thy creatures, O Lord, and renew Thy glory
        within us.
R.   Let not the breath be lost that glorifies our bodies,
        Let not the splendor be lost that glorifies our wisdom,
        Let not the law be lost that glorifies our freedom.
V.   Glory be to the Father, the Son, and the Holy Spirit,
R.   As was in the beginning, is now, and shall be forever.
                                        Amen.

Let us pray:
O God, Who made us first a little less than the angels,
Bound by Thy contract with clay to a certain measure of
splendor,

Gather and bring, we beseech Thee, Thy light to this riddle,
    Creator:
How, insecure in Thy gain from that lesser loan to our nature,
Thy Majesty dared the last risk of lending Its Face for refusal,
Secret unprayable vision; for Thine is the Life and the King-
    dom,
World without end.   *Amen.*

Blessing
God bless the working of the holy pen
Which writes the riddle of His ways with men.

LITTLE LESSON: *which is the Little
Chapter of None*

And the Lord God put man
In the garden of pleasure
To work and keep it,
And commanded him, saying:
"From every tree
Of the garden, eat.
But from the tree of knowledge
Of good and evil,
Do not eat.
For the day you eat
You shall die the death."

Benediction
God keep our understanding of the breath
    Which makes us wise and free,
And teach us in another Hour of death
    And the forbidden tree.
        Amen.

34

TIERCE

Hymn

Our tale goes dim with time and doubt,
    And Thou, O Spirit, must reveal
The garden gift, the broken trust,
    The lasting forfeit which we feel.

We know the garden of our prime
    Darkly in dreams and whisperings,
Remembering one boyhood hour
    Of wiser laughter, better things.

Father Who gave the garden gift,
    Son Who unclosed the gates again,
Revelation, Soul of God,
    Make the forgotten story plain.
              Amen.

Ant. And God said:

"I am not satisfied to make you brutal,
One brief mechanic spasm in the mire,
Leaving the cryptic constellations futile,
With life and lust the term of your desire.
I am not satisfied to make you human,
Learning by steps from cave to peak and star,
Training on sin and tragedy like freemen,
To spell and love Me from the things that are.
But I put revelation on your reason

35

And on your choices justice and My grace,
Till keeping faith and lowliness a season
You live to kiss and glorify My Face.
    Meanwhile I make a garden of this sod
    Not unbecoming men who look at God.

"I plant the garden: yours shall be the reaping,
All harmless trees that save and fortify,
The Tree of Life to heal the clay of sleeping,
But not the Tree of Knowledge, or you die.
That bitter wood will not allay your hunger,
Slake any thirst, or answer any need;
It cannot make you wiser, taller, younger—
Pride is the only passion it can feed.
That barren timber keeps no knowledge hidden;
No wisdom is denied you, small or whole—
One black sensation only is forbidden,
Experience of treason in the soul.
    For when you feel that wound of broken trust,
    Then God must bear your passion in your dust.

"Die beggar—and your heirs, not unprovided,
Will reckon planting moons and harvest suns
Till the last bearded prairie is divided
For treasure where the gleaming colter runs.
Die pauper—and your children will inherit
Sinew enough to crack the hills for gold,
Vision to launch armadas from a garret,
Stomach to storm the breaches or to hold.
But die with knowledge of this apple in you,
Explore the earth, forsake the dustless sky—
And all your sons footweary will continue
Forever wingless and condemned to fly.
    Two other covenants I make with men,
    But this one, broken, comes not whole again."

Ant. And God said: "But not the Tree of Knowledge, or you die."

LITTLE CHAPTER: *which is the Little
Chapter of Lauds*

And the Lord God formed man
Of the slime of the earth
And breathed into his face
The breath of life.
And man became a living soul.
And the Lord God had planted
A garden of pleasure from the beginning
Where He placed man whom He had formed.

LITTLE R.

*Show us the destiny, Father, **which Adam gives to
his children.
V.   Carry, Redeemer, the wound
**Which Adam gives to his children.
V.   Glory be to the Father, the Son, and the Holy Spirit.
*Show us the destiny, Spirit, **which Adam gives to
his children.

V.   Nations shall hear and rejoice in the happy sin of their
father;
R.   Kings shall listen and mourn for the unhappy boon of
redemption.

Let us pray:
Gather and bring, we beseech Thee, Thy light to this riddle,
Redeemer:
How we came first to the garden and then to the garden of
earth,

37

And why the fair lady of Eden is not the mother of life;
Thou Who art Life, and one King, and one God with the
  Father and Spirit,
World without end.   *Amen.*

SEXTE

HYMN

Our vision of Thy beauty, Lord,
  Is less from tall immortal skies
Than from the tenderness we feel
  For bended faces, dying eyes.

And more than to esteem of man
  To worship of a woman clings
Remembrance of a boyhood hour
  Of wiser laughter, better things.

Refashion, Father, what we break,
  Follow, Redeemer, where we stray,
And Thou, O Holy Spirit, send
  Thy beauty shining through the clay.
                                    Amen.

Ant. It is not good for man to be alone.

God knew the loneliness of Adam's gladness,
And, setting seal like harvest after dearth,
Touching our dawn like music out of sadness,
Came Eve to be the mother of the earth.
Then first man felt the beauty of a maiden
Bound the dim ocean of desire with shore:
The Polestar leads our breathless vessels laden
With hardy cargo home, but she leads more.
Then man, first reckless, yielded to another

More of his destiny than flesh can fill:
But, penitent or faithful, wife and mother,
She keeps our visions and our houses still.
    And God have mercy on them, who believe
      Worse of His daughters in the name of Eve.

Hers to be clean Diana in the moonlight,
Cecilia looking in the angel's eyes,
Elaine forsaken in the cold lagoon-light,
Miranda twinkling as her lover sighs.
Hers are the feet of Ruth and Martha's labor,
Esther's calm rightness in the royal hall;
Barbara smiling at the arching saber,
Joan flaming upright in the broken wall.
Hers to be Genevieve above the city,
Blanche at the cradle trembling on her knees,
Rachel in Rama, Brigid pale with pity;
Hers to be mother of the Macchabees.
    Almost, you fancy, Mary looks at you,
      Till Eve turns on you not one face, but two.

For she is Lilith, ageless adversary
To all allegiance which her wifehood earns,
And Helen dooming Priam's sanctuary,
Richest adornment of the house she burns.
She is fair Messalina in the palace
Barring with lust access to Caesar's ear,
Lucrezia laughing past the scented chalice,
Black Athaliah throned on blood and fear.
She is Delilah sometimes to her minion,
Sometimes Isolda in their double woe,
And sometimes after war such short dominion
Of Egypt as the conqueror shall know.
    Eve comes to judgment guilty, nor alone.
      Let him that is without sin cast the first stone.

Ant. It is not good for man to be alone, and God made Eve.

LITTLE CHAPTER: *Genesis 2, 23–24:*

And Adam said:
"She is bone of my bone
And flesh of my flesh.
So a man shall leave
Father and mother,
And cling to his wife.
They shall be two in one flesh."

LITTLE R.

*Show us, Creator, the boon **which earth receives of its mother.
V. Pardon, Redeemer, the wound
**Which earth receives of its mother.
V. Glory be to the Father, the Son, and the Holy Spirit.
*Show us, O Spirit, the boon **which earth receives of its mother.

V. Teach Thy people, O Lord, that woman was made for a blessing.
R. Let her walk among men in garments of goodness and mercy.

Let us pray:
Gather and bring, we beseech Thee, Thy light to this riddle, Redeemer:
How we came first to the garden and then to the garden of earth,
And why the Tree of Knowledge is not the Tree of Life;
Thou Who art Life, and one King, and one God with the Father and Spirit,
World without end. *Amen.*

41

NONE

Hymn

We cannot read Thy glory, Lord,
  As in the dawn Thy plan was laid,
Or run with Eve in innocence,
  Wide-eyed beneath the blameless shade.

We know at noon the garden gone,
  The portal coldly crossed with bars:
Darkness is never far from day,
  And earth an exile in the stars.

Bend, Father, Son, and Holy Ghost,
  Among Thy truer points of fire
And turn our outcast planet square
  Upon the land of our desire.
                              Amen.

Ant. Satan entered the serpent.

The Serpent said to Eve: "From the beginning
I am acquainted with the ways of God,
And yet I cannot understand what cunning
Leads Him to make a garden of this sod
And then, at odds with His own gift, discreetly
Caution you not to eat of every tree!"
But Eve, it may be, smiled to think how neatly
The simple truth discomfits sophistry
And said: "Your riddle, Serpent, is too sweeping.
We eat all trees that save and fortify,

The Tree of Life to heal the clay of sleeping,
But not the Tree of Knowledge—or we die.
    And *that* for Adam and his mate is reason
    Enough to shun all apples out of season."

The Serpent caught his tongue in hesitation;
But, side-long glancing, Eve invited more
And, flushed with confidence and confutation,
Lost the first battle of our oldest war.
The Serpent said: "No doubt your race will comment
Better on God and teach us in the end,
But we slow ancient creatures for the moment
Have surplus of experience to lend.
I learnt theology in a hard college
And you are welcome to it, though I see
You scarcely want my lecture, since the knowledge
Is freely yours for eating of the Tree.
    As to the Tree itself, as I conceive it,
    According to your pleasure take or leave it."

He said: "Divinity is not precisely
A kind of Being—but some high degree
Of self-esteem, some breadth of vision, nicely
Developing the personality.
Now, I once took the rougher road to godhead,
The way of self-esteem, but you were wise
To try for vision, which is first embodied
In good and evil known with open eyes.
As to the Tree, the warning God once uttered
Against your eating is itself a sign
You will not die, but have your eyes unshuttered
And, knowing good and evil, be divine."
    Eve took the fruit of knowledge to divide
    With Adam. And their eyes were opened wide.

Ant. Satan entered the serpent, and Adam ate of the
    Tree.

And the Lord God put man
In the garden of pleasure
To work it and keep it,
And commanded him, saying:
"From every tree
Of the garden eat.
But from the tree of knowledge
Of good and evil,
Do not eat.
For the day you eat
You shall die the death."

LITTLE R.

*Lord, it is afternoon. **Come down into the garden.
V.   God, the sun is declining.
    **Come down into the garden.
V.   Glory be to the Father, the Son, and the Holy Spirit.
    *Lord, it is afternoon. **Come down into the garden.

V.   Hasten Thy coming, Lord, for there is need of Thy coming.
R.   Thy people open their eyes on knowledge of good and of evil.

Let us pray:
Gather and bring, we beseech Thee, Thy light to this riddle, Redeemer:
How we came first to the garden and then to the garden of earth,
And why the promise of Satan is not the Promise of life;
Thou Who art Life, and one King, and one God with the Father and Spirit,
World without end.   *Amen.*

VESPERS

Ant 1. God went walking in paradise.

When God went walking, Eden stirred to greet Him:
Back from His feet the thicket lithely flowed,
The mildest breeze ran whispering to meet Him,
And slanting amber followed where He strode.
There, cloverblossoms learnt their way of massing
Where trails divide the field or rim the hill;
The jungle keeps memorial of His passing
In vaulted tunnels through the timber still.
The vulture paused on his eternal mission,
The blindest burrow opened to the sky,
Wings and alert bright eyes forgot suspicion:
There was no loneliness where God went by.
    But God, gone walking, has no tryst with these—
    No one He seeks is moving in the trees.

Ant. God went walking in paradise, and they hid
    from the face of the Lord.
Ant. 2. God called them forth.

Then He reproached them: "Why should a child go
    fleeing
The only Face that never meant him harm
Unless forbidden fruit has taught his being
Sight of first shame and tingle of alarm?"

But, willing to be justified, our father
Answered and not as one who loved his mate:

"The woman that You gave to help me, rather
Tempted me with the apple and I ate."
So, in his turn, he scandalized the woman
Who first seduced him, teaching Eve her plea:
"Adam is in me. I am only human.
The Snake deceived me and I ate the Tree."
    And only Satan had no word to say,
    Wrapped in his silence after his judgment day.

Ant. God called them forth, and they accused the
      Serpent.
Ant. 3. God cursed the Serpent.

Forbearing then to quench the smoking ember
Or tread the splintered reed, He rather gave,
Cursing the Snake, one Promise to remember
On winter nights, long after, in the cave.
But, cursing Eve, He spoke of tribulation:
"Because you swayed the man against My law,
You shall be under Adam's domination
To hold his silence and command in awe.
Your only hope and Promise for tomorrow
Is in your children—see they be not few.
You shall conceive and bring them forth in sorrow,
Who, born and dying, lay their grief on you.
    But you shall guard the Promise in My name,
    Beneath your harder curse, to Adam's shame."

Ant. God cursed the Serpent, and made the Promise.
Ant. 4. God cursed Adam:

"Because you find the voice of Eve entreating
Stronger to sway you than My plain command
And taste the Tree not given for your eating,
Curst be the earth beneath your weary hand.
Labor and toil reluctantly shall earn you
Not many years dividing death from birth,

But thorns and thistles shall the ground return you
And you shall eat the grasses of the earth.
Sweat of your brow shall bitterly be shaken
Upon the bread you eat, till you be thrust
Into the earth from which you first were taken:
For dust you are and shall return to dust."
 Then God cast Adam out and fiercely barred
 Eden with lightning and an angel guard.

Ant. God cursed Adam, and cast him out.
Ant. 5. Lightning.

In the beginning God prepared a garden,
Setting us there to cherish it or spurn,
And all our thought of Arcady and Arden
Is for that Eden which will not return.
Beach of our exile never fails of fairness:
The night we walk into is fair with eyes,
Wavering wasteland drenches golden bareness
Fairly with purple lapsing from the skies,
Fair the proud-headed thistle stands immortal,
Fair with our weeping calls the whippoorwill,
And I, despite of lightning in the portal,
Know that my way is through a garden still.
 But in the rainbow of the sun I see
 My garden bare its thorns, and wait for me.

Ant. Lightning and an angel guard.

Little Chapter: Genesis 3, 23–24:

  And the Lord God sent Adam
  Out of the garden of pleasure
  To till the earth
  From which he was taken,
  And He placed at the garden

47

Cherubim and a flaming sword
Turning all directions,
To keep the way
Of the Tree of Life.

Hymn

High Word of Heaven, come of old
  Out of the timeless Father's breast,
Born to the rescue of a world
  Whose sun has fallen to the west,

Brighten our bosoms with Thy light
  And burn them empty with Thy love,
Till, free of all that dies below,
  They brim with laughter from above.

So, when the Judge upon His throne
  Pays all destroyers off in fire
But calls the faithful each by name
  And gives them heaven for their hire,

We may not headlong feed the pool
  Where black tornados flame and nod,
But glory in the happy sky,
  Co-owners of the Face of God.

As to the Father, as to Son,
  O Holy Spirit, so to Thee,
The glory of all ages past
  Be Thine in ages yet to be.
                    Amen.

V.   Come, Heaven, down in dew: and rain
        The Holy One to earth.

R.   Lay open, Land, the bursting plain:
And bring the Savior forth.

Ant. Behold the Promise of God.

CANTICLE OF THE PROMISE

My spirit calls the Lord Magnificent:
His anger saves, His very curse is mild,
And woman's long atonement all is bent
To consummation in a blameless Child.
Such Promise needs a Mother undefiled,
Though only guilty race needs such a Son,
Guilty until indeed that miracle be done.

Ant. Behold the Promise of God comes from far off,
and the brightness of Him fills the round world.

Let us pray:
Gather and bring, we beseech Thee, Thy light to this riddle,
Redeemer:
How we came first to the garden and then to the garden of
earth,
And how Thy Promise will come and save us from exile to life;
Thou Who art Life, and one King, and one God with the
Father and Spirit,
World without end.   *Amen.*

COMPLINE

Blessing
Favor us, Lord Omnipotent, and send
A night of silence and a perfect end.

LITTLE LESSON: *1 Peter 5, 8–9:*

Be sober, keep watch!
For your adversary the devil
Goes about like a roaring lion,
Hunting someone to devour.
But stand him off,
Strong in faith.

God is our strength, the same that made the sky:
Except in Him we till the earth and die.
His home is more than Eden, but the door
Is through that garden where we come no more.
His be the Judgment: we confess to Him
We have deserved the sword and Cherubim.
His grace will quicken and His justice wait,
Till heaven opens on a second gate;
His mercy sudden and His anger slow,
With Promise of a second way to go;
His own atonement turns away His wrath,
His deed of ransom points our second path.

Ant. And Eve said:

"Adam, the black of night and bitter weather
Crowd in upon the fire, the bread is thin,

Abel and Cain walk warily together,
But God consoled me when He cursed my sin.
He might that day have quenched the smoking ember
And trod the splintered reed; instead He gave,
Cursing the Snake, a Promise to remember
On nights like these unhappy in the cave.
Cursing the Snake, He said: *Among all cattle*
You shall be lowest. Stinging dust shall cleave
To jaw and belly of you. Dust of battle
I put between you and the sons of Eve.
    You will lie waiting for the woman's tread,
    But with a Manchild she shall crush your head.

"And that day when it comes will melt the mountains
To drops of sweetness and the hills will flow
With milk and honey, unforbidden fountains
Where seekers thirsty for the Lord may go.
A Prophet comes, appointed for atonement:
He breaks the gate and puts the garden right.
A Master comes, anointed for enthronement:
The Saints are with Him and He brings the light.
Adam, night passes, time will come for waking,
Rescue is not so far away as when
We heard the Promise first. Dawn will be breaking,
We shed the night, we dress for daylight then.
    Soon, we will walk with honor in the sun,
    Clad in the Hope of the Anointed One.

"Adam, I wonder, knowing Cain and Abel,
If any boy of mine will be the One,
Or if some daughter, when the clouds of fable
Close over you and me, will bear that Son.
How many girls have I condemned, I wonder,
To agony which you can never know,
Prolonging hope, until they too go under
With common anguish in the earth below?

I wonder how that Boy can be the brother
Of breed in whom the blood of Adam runs,
And what bright maiden better than her mother
Will justify the hope we have in sons.
  But all the Serpent's conquest and design
  Will come to nothing in some Child of mine."

Ant. And Eve said: "He will come."

Hymn

Reckon it not too foolish, Lord,
  That we must paint the morning sun
Across the shadow of the world
  Even when night has just begun.

For we remember Thy defence
  Mostly keenly where the demons roam,
And houses which let darkness in
  Remind us of another home.

Father and Founder of the sky,
  Only-begotten Truth and Light,
Spirit and kindly Beacon-Ray,
  Lead us to Eden in the night.
                              Amen.

Little Chapter: *Jeremias 14, 8:*

Savior in time of trouble!
Why wilt Thou be as a stranger,
A stranger in the land,
And as a wayfaring man
Turning in for lodging?

Little R.

*Into Thy keeping, O Lord, **we commend our search
  for a Savior.

52

V.   God of Redemption and Truth,
    **We commend our search for a Savior.

V.   Glory be to the Father, the Son, and the Holy Spirit.
    *Into Thy keeping, O Lord, **we commend our search
      for a Savior.

V.   He guards us as the apple of His eye,
R.   Under the shadow of His wings we fly.

Ant. Save us, Lord.

Canticle of the Expectation

Dismiss us never from Thy service, Lord,
Till by Thy Promise we may go in peace—
Until our eyes have seen the Saving Word
When Thou hast made Him ready for the face
Of nations: Light of Revelation shown
To other lands and Glory of His own.

Ant. Save us, Lord: we wait in the night.

Prayers

Blessing Thy name the Office is begun,
Believing that our Savior is Thy Son;
Blessing Thy story all the Hours are tended,
Blessing Thy glory Work and day are ended:
And blessing Thee the spinning ages run
The bright itinerary of the sun;
For sky in sky has impetus to gear it
Forward on praise of Father, Son, and Spirit.

And He will bless *us* for His mercy's sake
Resting, because in Him we rise and wake,
And measure when the sun is sloping dim

53

His pity by the hope we have in Him.
He will put watch upon the night and keep
The stars from wandering and us asleep.
Our prayer of praise is heard;
Our cry comes to the Lord.

Let us pray:

Visit the house, we beseech Thee, that welcomes Redemption,
    O Father;
Far from it parry the conquest and all the designs of the Ser-
    pent;
Make Thy angel dwell in it to keep us in peace; and Thy
    blessing
Come down upon us forever; through Jesus Christ our Re-
    deemer,
Who is one Life, and one King, and one God with Thee and
    the Spirit,
World without end.   *Amen.*

BENEDICTION

God grant we fold the book, as hands, at nightfall
    Turning to better prayers, and unaghast
Set in the dark our faces to the frightful
    Return of sleep, as all men must at last.
Ready or anxious, we approach the mystery
    Of night in ignorance, as men wait death,
Like Adam leaving Eden, when our history
    Was all before him, with expectant breath.
But God Who kept him when he faltered most
Will guard us, Father, Son, and Holy Ghost.
                                Amen.

LAST ANTIPHON: TO MARY

Dear Mother of the Savior, yet remaining
Star of the Sea and heaven's open door,
Come when we stumble, lifting and sustaining,
For in our hearts we long to rise once more.
You who, defying nature, still continue
Virgin before and after Gabriel's call,
You who, defying nature, wrought the sinew
Of Him Who made you, pity us who fall.

V.   Eve's angel keeps a garden ringed with fire,
R.   But Mary's angel answers Eve's desire.

Let us pray:
Pour, we beseech Thee, O Lord, the flood of Thy grace on
    our spirits,
That, as by an angel's voice we have known of Thy Son's
    Incarnation,
So by His Passion and Cross we may be led through to the
    glory
Of rising again from the dead: through the same Jesus Christ
    our Redeemer. *Amen.*

FOR THE FIRST SUNDAY IN ADVENT
explicit

AFTER THE HOURS

Now to the Holy and Invested Trinity,
 Unmingled, undivided, Three in One:
To the immortal crucified Humanity
 Of Lord and brother, Jesus Christ the Son:
To the unaltered, fruitful, whole Virginity
 Of Mary, first in grace and first in praise:
And to the free and pre-ordained community
 Of all the Saints, may every creature raise
Music of glory, vast as all infinity,
 And we who made these Hours—healed of wrong
And all our sins forgiven—with impunity
 Come to the making of that greater song.
          Amen.